The Kevin Roth Children's Songbook

ISBN 0-931759-97-8
SAN 683-8022

Typesetting - Derek Cornett
Transcribing - George Ports
Cover Art - Elinor Kaslow
Paste-up - Cindy Middlebrook

CENTERSTREAM Publishing
P.O. Box 5450 - Fullerton CA 92635

Contents

Foreword

B. Proud Photography

Kevin Roth

Nearly a decade ago, I recorded my first children's record in a tiny studio located in back of my friend Ola Belle Reed's home. It was so small, that while one musician was recording his part, the rest of the band was outside playing Frisbee.

Ola Belle told me way back then that with every performance, recording, and audience I sang to, I would be planting a seed with my music. Little did I know that those words went from her mouth to God's ears. The letters, pictures, and friends that have come my way over the years, have surprised me and inspired me the most. I never imagined any of this success for myself. It's been quite a journey.

I have a career recording and performing for "adults" as well, yet it seems that the children'/family music has brought me the most attention so far. It took me a long time to understand why.

There is a child in all of us just waiting to come out and "be." In today's world, so complex, so high tech, our "inner child" or "soul" is thirsty for simplicity, unconditional love, acceptance, and comfort in knowing all is well. I never recognized this consciously, but as my life has evolved it has become clear that we are all on a similar path walking side-by-side with our "inner child."

The songs I write for children have always spoken to this "inner child." It wasn't until parents came up to me at concerts or wrote me letters telling me how much my music has moved them and their children that I realized I was singing to everyone, not just the little folk. Through my music, the adults remembered the innocence of their childhood, its simplicity, and its fun. They wanted to feel it again, desperately.

Many thanks are due to some people who have helped me bring these moments to you. Linda Katz, Rick Sigglekow, Jack Roth, Grant Birchard, Chris Knowles, Patrick Andrews, Donna Zimmerman, Jill Haley, Lisa Raho, Marshall Toppo, Linda Morganstern-Robbins Moses Asch, Ola Belle, Bud, and Dave Reed, Peter Yarrow, Noel Paul Stookey, Mary Travers, and all the others who have helped create the dream.

Along the way there have been many exciting times. Some of the highlights of my career have been: singing the T.V. theme "Shining Time Station," receiving numerous American Library Association Awards, and the Parent's Choice Award, giving two concerts at the White House, receiving wonderful reviews in national magazines, singing a duet of the classic *"Puff The Magic Dragon"* with my long-time friend Peter Yarrow, appearing on Eureeka's Castle, having books and tapes published by Random House, and countless other surprises.

In the end, of all the accolades, it has been the simple words, "planting a seed," that has meant the most to me.

I still record in "tiny studios." I write my music in a sunny house often laughing at ideas that come through me and onto paper. Sometimes I cry when words and music come to me that seem to heal my inner child as they are written. My words and music have always come together at the same time, one cushioning the other. Life is indeed a journey, a process as it unfolds.

I hope these songs make your travels a bit sweeter, they are some of my favorites. Sing them with joy. Teach them to your children. By doing this you too will help spread the seed in song and spirit.

Kevin Roth

The Singing Dragon

by Kevin Roth

Chorus
I'm gonna go where the sun's always shining.
There's a magic song I love to sing.
I learned the words from the singing dragon.
Who takes you there on musical wings.

"I know a place" said the singing dragon,
"it's over the rainbow and far above,
All of your problems, all of your sorrows,
the only way there is through the song of love."
Now all of the animals and all of the people
live together in this land.
Monkeys play the music, gorillas lead the
chorus & the laughing hyenas conducted the band.

Chorus

Now the singing dragon gathered a chorus,
from fish in the ocean to birds in the trees.
Big dinosaurs and little bitty critters all sang
together in harmony.
When the storm-cloud came the singing dragon
struck up the band for a chorus or two.
The storm-cloud heard the song about love,
and blew away to let the sun shine through.

Chorus

Oh, sing to me, oh musical dragon
Sing to me a song I know.
One that makes you feel good all over.
From deep in your heart down to your toes.

So if you're feeling sad or even lonely
The singing dragon has a song for you.
It's a song of love that makes you feel happy.
When you sing it with others, you feel good too.

Chorus (repeat twice)

My first performance, Kevin and sister Jill

Down By The Bay

Traditional/new words & music by Kevin Roth

The Professor

This is a lot of fun to sing. I'd like to dedicate this to Vincent Price, Bela Lugosi, and all the other scary men that spook us, and give us goose bumps!

by Kevin Roth

Chorus
Bones, bones a million bones, big ones, small ones,
who would have known.
The crazy professor would have grown dinosaurs
right in his home.

The storm blew hard, the rain came down.
He put on his mask and his doctor gown.
The lightning cracked, the thunder roared.
He laid the bones all over the floor.
Bone by bone all through the night
He built dinosaurs in the pale moonlight.
Some were huge and ugly, some were cute and small.
The crazy man built them all.

Chorus

It's been a few million years or more
Since anybody's seen a real dinosaur.
I know it sounds a little strange to you
But when the lightning struck and the storm blew there were . . .

Chorus (repeat twice)

That Bear Makes Me Crazy

One of the many crazy songs from my recording "Unbearable Bears"

by Kevin Roth

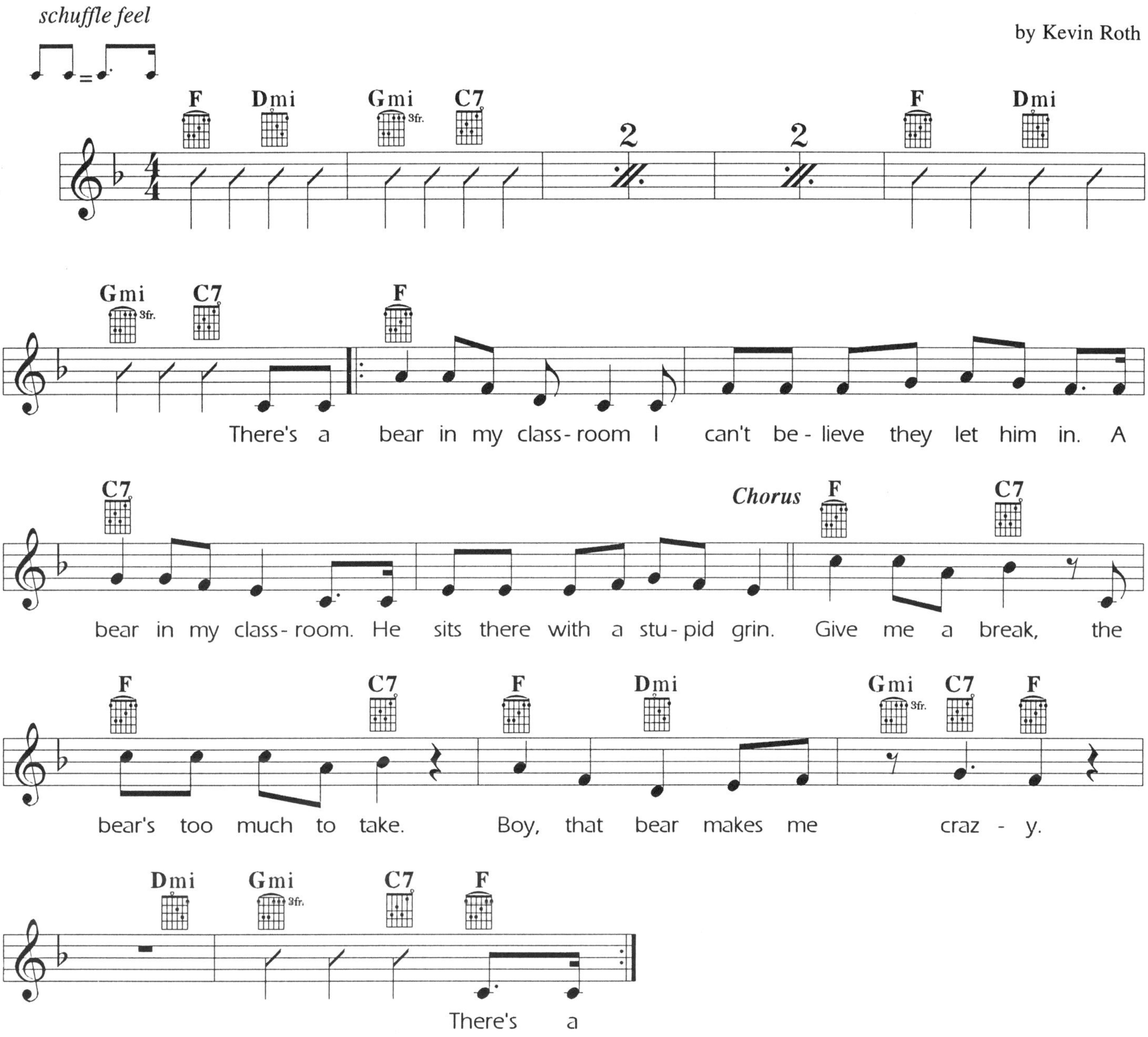

There's a bear in my classroom
I can't believe they let him in
A bear in my classroom
He sits there with a stupid grin

Chorus
Give me a break
The bear's too much to take
Boy, that bear makes me crazy

There's a bear on the school bus
I can't believe they let him on
A bear on the school bus
Every day he rides along

Chorus

There's a bear at the school dance
I can't believe they let him go
A bear in the school dance
The Romeo of bear romance

Chorus

There's a bear in the lunchroom
I can't believe he eats with me
A bear in the lunchroom
A most disgusting sight to see

Chorus

Now, there's a bear on the ball team
I can't believe they let him play
A bear on the ball team
When he comes get out of his way

Chorus (repeat 3 times)

The Snoring Bear

by Kevin Roth

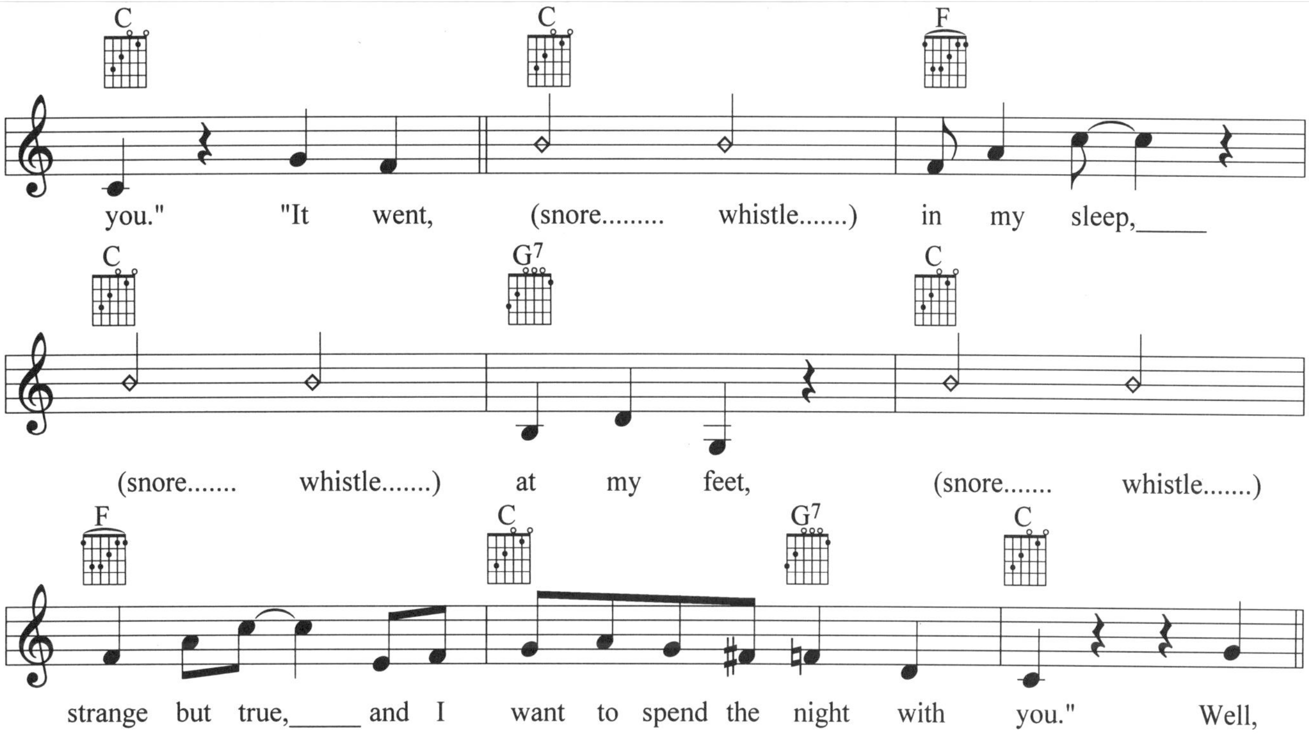

The bear came in the other night
And he turned on the bedroom light
Scared and shaken as can be
He said, "Oh won'cha spend the night with me"
He said, "the moon was full and the stars were bright
When I heard a noise in the wind tonight
Strangest noise I ever knew
And I want I want to spend the night with you"

Chorus
"It went (snore...whistle) in my sleep
(snore...whistle) at my feet
(snore...whistle) strange but true
And I want to spend the night with you"

"Well, climb in bed", I said to him
We pulled the covers to our chin
When I heard that funny noise begin
And I want to spend the night with you

Chorus

Well, the noise grew louder in my ear
And I screamed, " hey bear, the noise is here"
When he woke up, it disappeared
And I want to spend the night with you

Chorus

The noise was coming from my bed
When I found it was, the bear instead
Just snoring from his hairy head
And I want to spend the night with you

Now a grizzly bear is fine I'm sure
A polar bear I like much more
But I don't like a bear that snores
And wants to spend the night with me

He goes (snore...whistle) in my sleep
(snore...whistle) at my feet
(snore...whistle) strange but true
I don't want to spend the night
And I don't want to spend the night with you.

I Know An Old Lady Who Swallowed A Fly

by Rose Bonne & Alan Mills

(Additional verses)

5.
I know an old lady who swallowed a dog,
She was a hog to swallow a dog.
She swallowed the dog to catch the cat,
She swallowed th cat to catch the bird,
She swallowed the bird to catch the spider,
That wriggled and juggled and fiddled inside her;
I don't know why she swallowed the fly.
Perhaps she'll die.

6.
I know an old lady who swallowed a goat,
Opened her throat and swallowed a goat.
She swallowed the goat to catch the dog,
She swallowed the dog to catch the cat, etc...

7.
I know an old lady who swallowed a cow,
I don't know how she swallowed a cow.
She swallowed the cow to catch the goat,
She swallowed the goat to catch the dog,
She swallowed the dog to catch the cat, etc...

You Are You

We are all different.
This song speaks for our rights to individuality, acceptance, and unconditional love.

by Kevin Roth

Chorus
You are you and I am me
No one is the same you see
We're all made so differently
And the world goes round and round

Yes, even skies are never the same
First it's sunny and then it rains
Flowers bloom and seasons change
And the world goes round and round

Chorus

Some kids grow up on city streets
Some on farms with corn and wheat
Some on boats that sail the seas
And the world goes round and round
Yes...

Chorus

But the one thing that we all share
Is the need for love, someone to care
Just to know that you are there
Helps my world go round
Yes...

Chorus

Noah's Ark

My favorite line in this song is the very last.
Noah, with a sense of humor!

by Kevin Roth

F7
B♭7
kang - a - roo, Pea - cocks, pos - sums,
F7
cam- els and crows, El - e- phants swing - in from their big long nose. Gor -
C7
F7
ill - as, Guin - ies, ham - sters and hens, chick - a - dees, wall - a - bies and
C7
To Chorus
F
big old wrens. Well it rained all day and it rained all night I
F7
B♭7
hard - ly saw an - y land in sight when No - ah said good
F
Lord we're here and two by two they all dis - a - peared.
C7
scat - tered through the world No - ah said good - bye He said it's
F
To Chorus
been a good trip I hope you all stay dry.

Mr. Bed Bug

by Kevin Roth

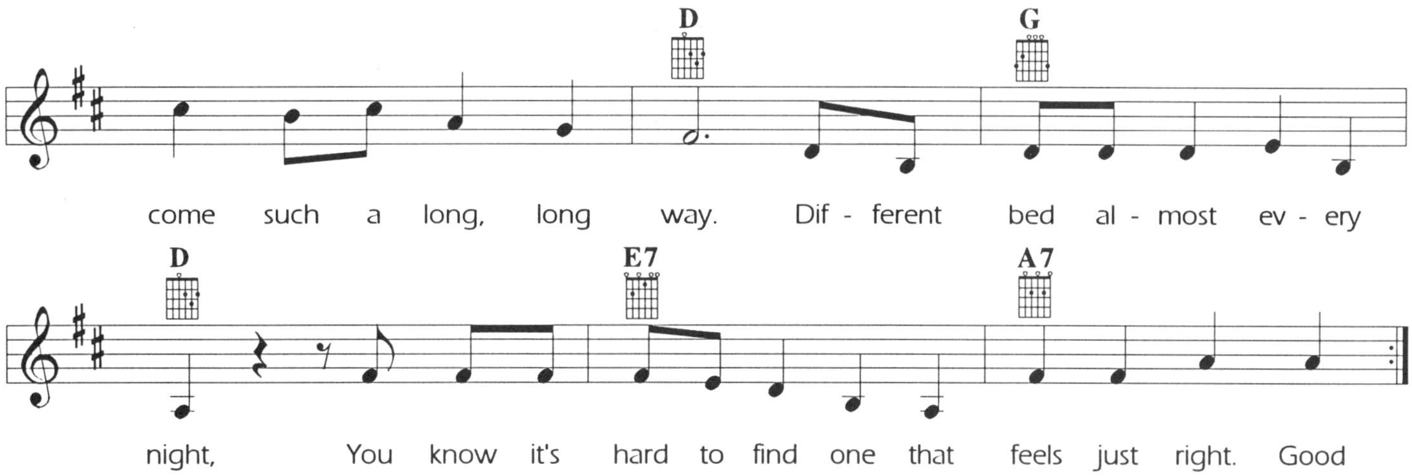

Chorus
Good night Mr. Bedbug, good night
I hope that you sleep tight
I hope that the people don't bite
Good night Mr. Bedbug, good night

"You see I've traveled from town to town
For a bedbug I get around
Oh I wish I had my very own bed
but every night it's someone else's instead
I hope you don't mind if I stay.
You know I've come such a long, long way.
A different bed most every night
You know it's hard to find one that feels just right."

Chorus

He said, "People can be so mean
When I snuggle they start to scream
slapping on the old bed sheets
just trying to put the squish on me
If you'd be so kind I'd like to stay
if you won't mind"
And so we snuggled the whole night through
The nicest bedbug I ever knew

Chorus

In the morning he said good-bye
And with a little wink of his eye
off he leaped in a single jump
and left me with a kiss and a big red rump

Chorus

My love affair and friendship with Peter, Paul and Mary has gone on for years. Here, I'm performing at the Valley Forge Music Fair in Devon, PA during Mary Traver's solo part of their concert. I was nervous, thrilled and completely blown away.

The Ladybug And The Moon

Of all the kids songs I have written, this is my very favorite. I sing it for adults too, because it's meaning is all about love in the 90's! It is now being illustrated as my first children's book.

by Kevin Roth

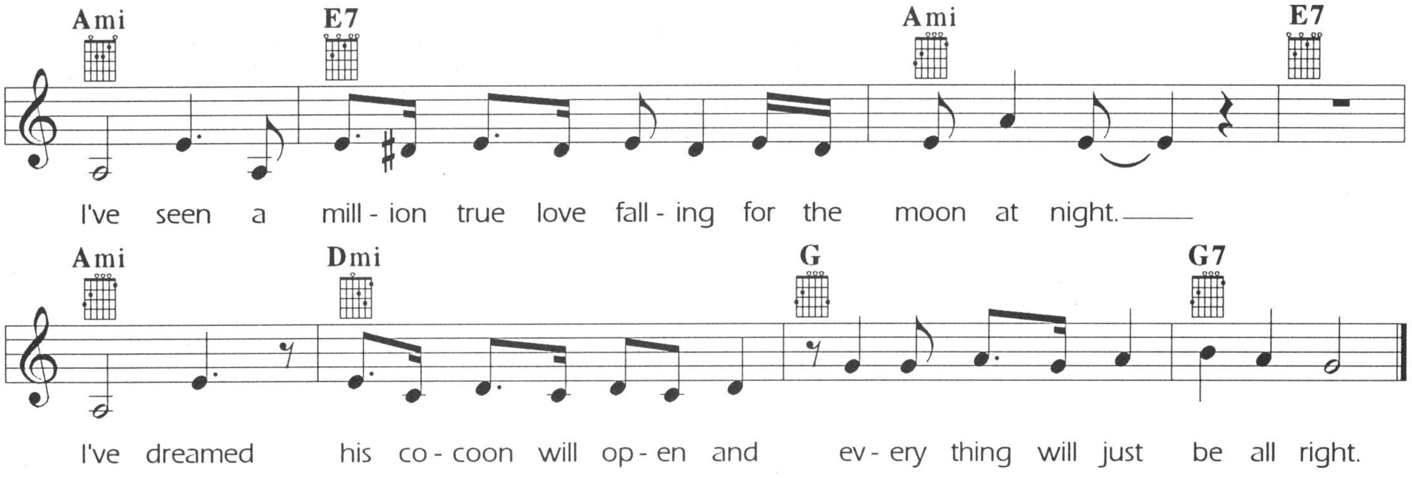

Hey, little ladybug
What are you dreamin' of
Watchin' the world go by
Sittin' right beside her
Was old Mr. Spider
Weaving a web with a wink in his eye

Chorus
But she only loves the big bugs
The ones that give her big hugs
The ones that fly through the sky
And she's looking for a mister
But can't find one that fits her
Oh, Lady Bug, don't cry

Now Mr. Grasshopper
He thought that he could stop her
From falling in love with the moon
He tried to explain
It's not a bug, it's got no brains
But she thinks it's Romeo's cocoon

Chorus

She said I've seen a million true love
Falling for the moon at night
And I've dreamed . . .
His cocoon will open
And everything will just be all right

Chorus

Now I heard she got married
To a cock-a-roach that carried
her off to his flat in L.A.
Living with the movie stars
work-outs, granola bars
not a bad life some say
But every night she dreams
of another bug it seems
one that crawls her way
Still staring at the moon
she waits for the big cocoon
to open up and carry her away

Chorus

Kevin and Shari Lewis at a White House performance, Washington D. C.
I think I'm asking Shari for Lamchop's hand in marriage.

Mr. Rabbit

Traditional/new words & music by Kevin Roth

Mr. Rabbit, Mr. Rabbit your ears are mighty long
"Yeah don't you know they were put on wrong"

Chorus
Every little soul's gonna shine, shine
Every little soul's gonna shine, along

Mr. Rabbit, Mr. Rabbit your fur's mighty white
"Yeah don't you know it keeps me warm at night"

Chorus

Mr. Rabbit, Mr. Rabbit your nose always twitches
"Yeah come sundown it always itches"

Chorus

Mr. Rabbit, Mr. Rabbit where do you sleep at night?
"Under the moon and stars shining bright"

Chorus

Mr. Rabbit, Mr. Rabbit what's your favorite dream?
"Well, carrots and parsnips and garden greens."

Chorus (twice)

Animal Fair

Traditional/new words & music by Kevin Roth

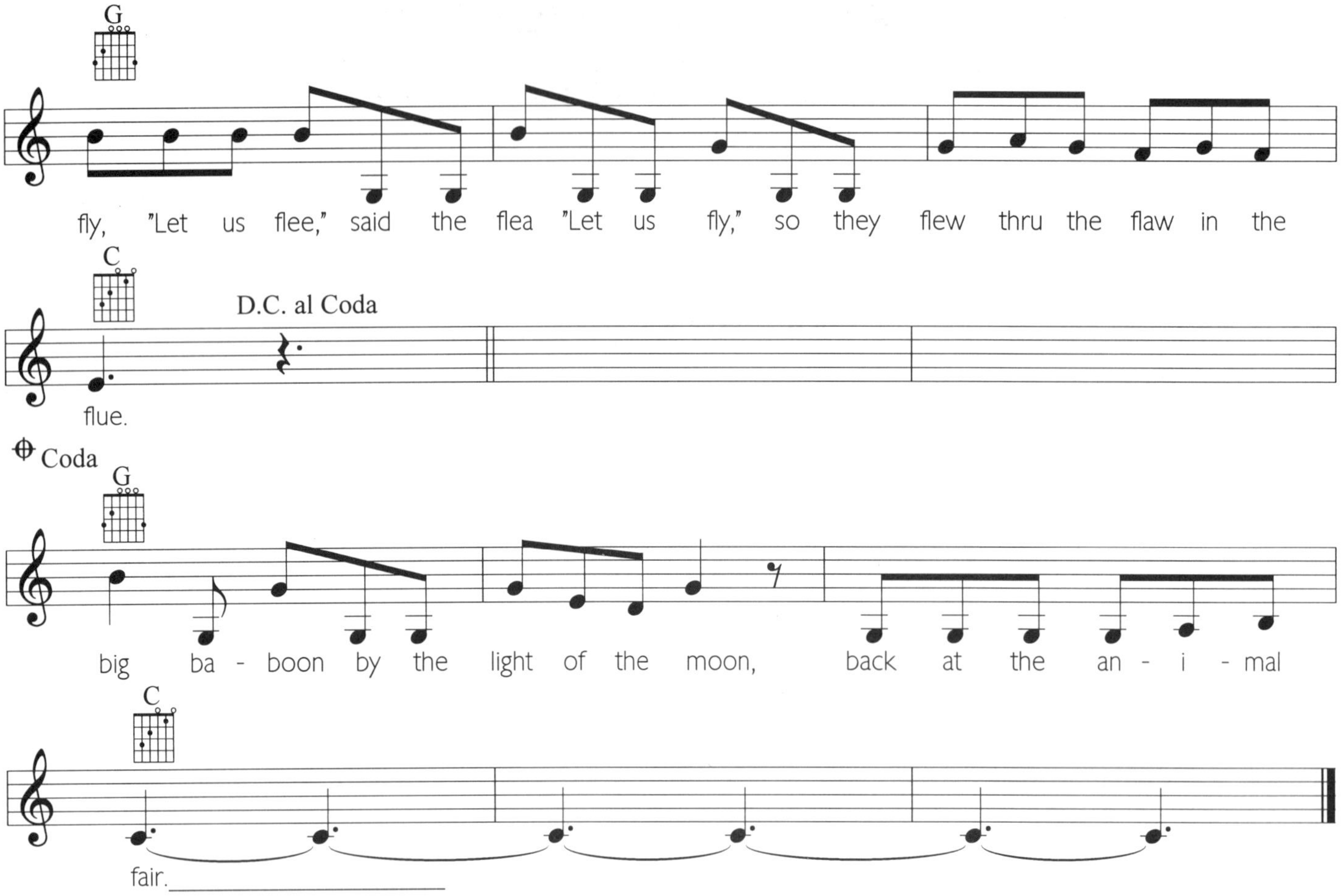

I went to the Animal Fair
The birds and the bees were there
The big baboon by the light of the moon was combing his auburn hair
The monkey he got drunk, and sat on the elephants trunk
The elephant sneezed and fell on his knees
And that was the end of the monk

Said a flea to a fly in a flue
"Oh flea what can we do"?
Said the fly let us flee, said the flea let us fly
So they flew thru the flaw in the flue

Back at the Animal Fair, the birds and the bees were there
The big baboon by the light of the moon
Was combing his auburn hair

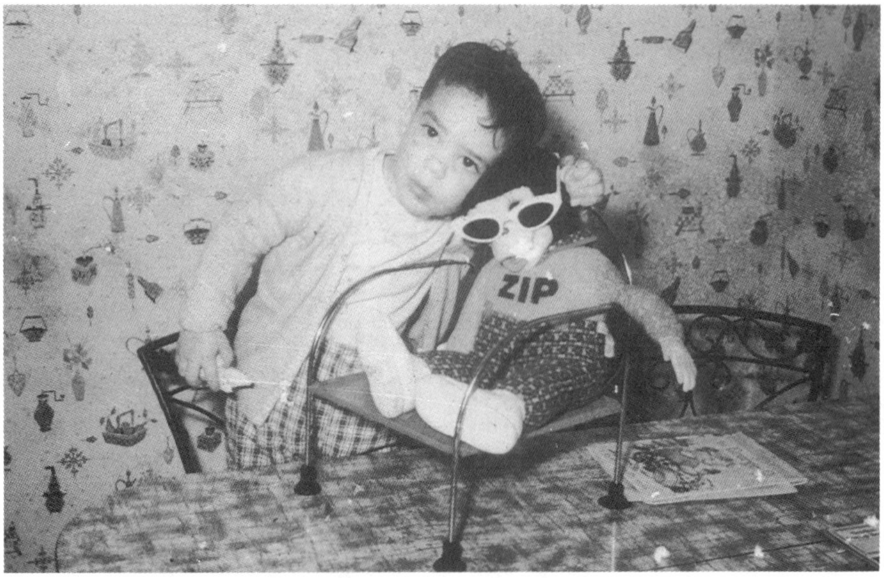

My childhood friend, Zippy

The Green Grass Grows All Around

Traditional/new words & music by Kevin Roth

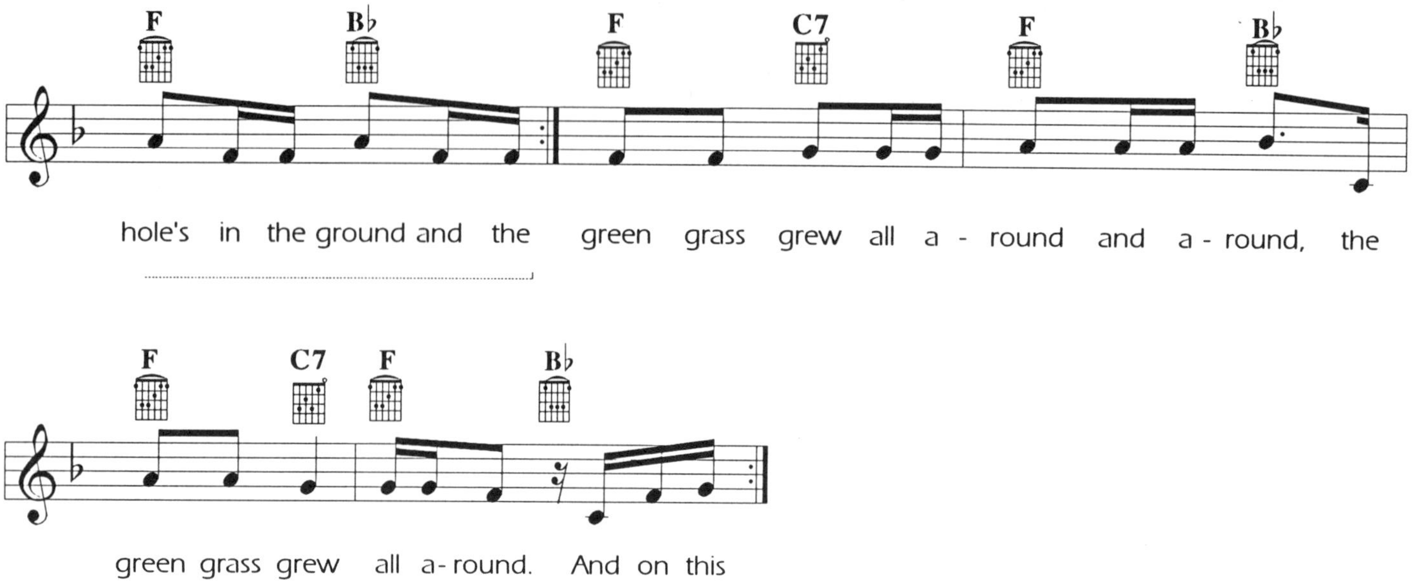

The verses are built progressively.

Use the continuous repeat section for the
music to repeat the progression from feather to root.

Ex: (final verse)
Well the feathers' on the wing, (repeat section)
The wings' on the bird,
The birds' in the egg, (repeat section)
The eggs' in the nest, etc...

My father and me at my first White House Concert. Washington, D.C.

I've Been Working On The Railroad
She'll Be Coming 'Round The Mountain

Traditional/new words & music by Kevin Roth

F G7 C
Di - nah won't ya' blow, Di - nah won't ya' blow your horn. You know there's
some - one in the kit - chen with Di - nah, some - one's in the kit - chen I
G7 C F
know, I know, some - one's in the kit - chen with Di - nah,
G7 C
strum - in' on the old ban - jo. They go fe, fi,
G7
fid - dle - e - i - o fe, fi, fid - dle - e - i - o - o - o - o -
C F G7
fe, fi, fid dle-e - i - o, strum - in' on the old ban -
C F
jo. She'll be com- in' 'round the

I've been working on the railroad all the live long day
I've been working on the railroad, just to pass the time away
Can't you here the whistle blowin', rise up early in the morn'
Can't you hear the whistle blowin', "Dinah Blow Your Horn"
Dinah won't you blow, Dinah won't you blow, Dinah won't you blow your horn.
Dinah won't you blow, Dinah won't you blow, Dinah won't you blow your horn.

You know someone's in the kitchen with Dinah, someone's in the kitchen I know,
Someone's in the kitchen with Dinah strumming on the old Banjo
They go , fe, fi fiddle-i-o, fe, fi fiddle-i-o, fe, fi fiddle-i-o
Strumming on the old banjo.

She'll be coming round the mountain when she comes
She'll be coming round the mountain when she comes
She'll be coming round the mountain,
She'll be coming round the mountain
She'll be coming round the mountain when she comes

She'll be riding six white horses when she comes
She'll be riding six white horses when she comes
She'll be riding six white horses,
She'll be riding six white horses
She'll be riding six white horses, when she comes.

We'll all go out to meet her when she comes
We'll all go out to meet her when she comes
We'll all go out to meet her, we'll all go out to meet her
We'll all go out to meet her when she comes

We'll all have chicken and dumplings when she comes
We'll all have chicken and dumplings when she comes
We'll all have chicken and dumplings,
We'll all have chicken and dumplings
We'll all have chicken and dumplings when she comes

She'll be coming round the mountain when she comes
She'll be coming round the mountain when she comes
She'll be coming round the mountain,
She'll be coming round the mountain
She'll be coming round the mountain when she comes

Here she comes . . .

The Wonder Song

Isn't it true?

by Kevin Roth

Why does the sun come out some days?
Sometimes clouds get in the way
Why do some people laugh and some just cry?
This old world never makes up its mind

Chorus
Oh I wonder, wonder why the world's so crazy but we all get by
I keep wondering, wondering why?

Some say it's good to be kind
But good people are getting mighty hard to find
I wish that love was as big as the world is round
Then everywhere I looked, love could be found

Chorus (repeat twice)

The moon is bright and the stars are surely warm
Every minute, some little baby is born
Born in love that will last their whole life through
I could sure use a little love how about you?

Chorus (repeat twice)

Little Piggy

by Judy Goodenough

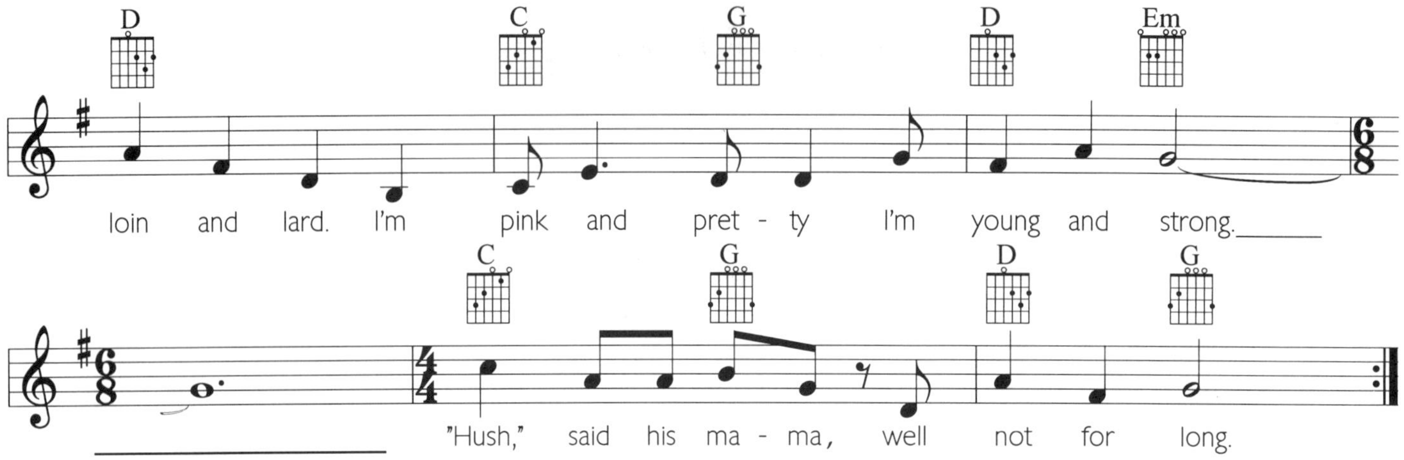

Little piggy hollered in the middle of the night
"Tell me Mama I gotta get it right
What'll I be when I get big?"
"Hush," said his mama, "you're gonna be a pig."

Chorus
That's how it is when you get older
You're bacon butt and picnic shoulder
All my sons and all my daughters
Are hocks and hams and tails and trotters

"Oh no," said the piggy, "that's mighty hard
There's more to me than loin and lard
I'm pink and pretty, I'm young and strong
"Hush," said his Mama, "well not for long.""

Chorus

"Oh no," said the piggy and started to howl
There's more to me than cheek and jowl
I walk and talk, I can sing and dance
"Now hush," said Mama, "You'll never get your chance."
"Not me," said piggy, "I'll show you all."
He went under the fence and climbed over the wall
He ran and he ran till the moon went down
He ran and he ran till he came to a town

Chorus

With a kink in his tail and a wink in his eye
He put on a suit and he put on his tie
He parted his hair and bought a diamond ring
And no one noticed anything
"Now see," said the piggy, "I'm one of you."
And everyone said, "How true, how true."
He made his money and he lives in style
And sometimes sings with half a smile

Chorus

He's a big boar now, an executive pork
He eats his vittles with a knife and fork
But still remembers that lonesome tune
That his Mama sang by the light of the moon

Chorus

Me and Mr. Rabbit

Bye-N-Bye

Traditional/arranged by Kevin Roth

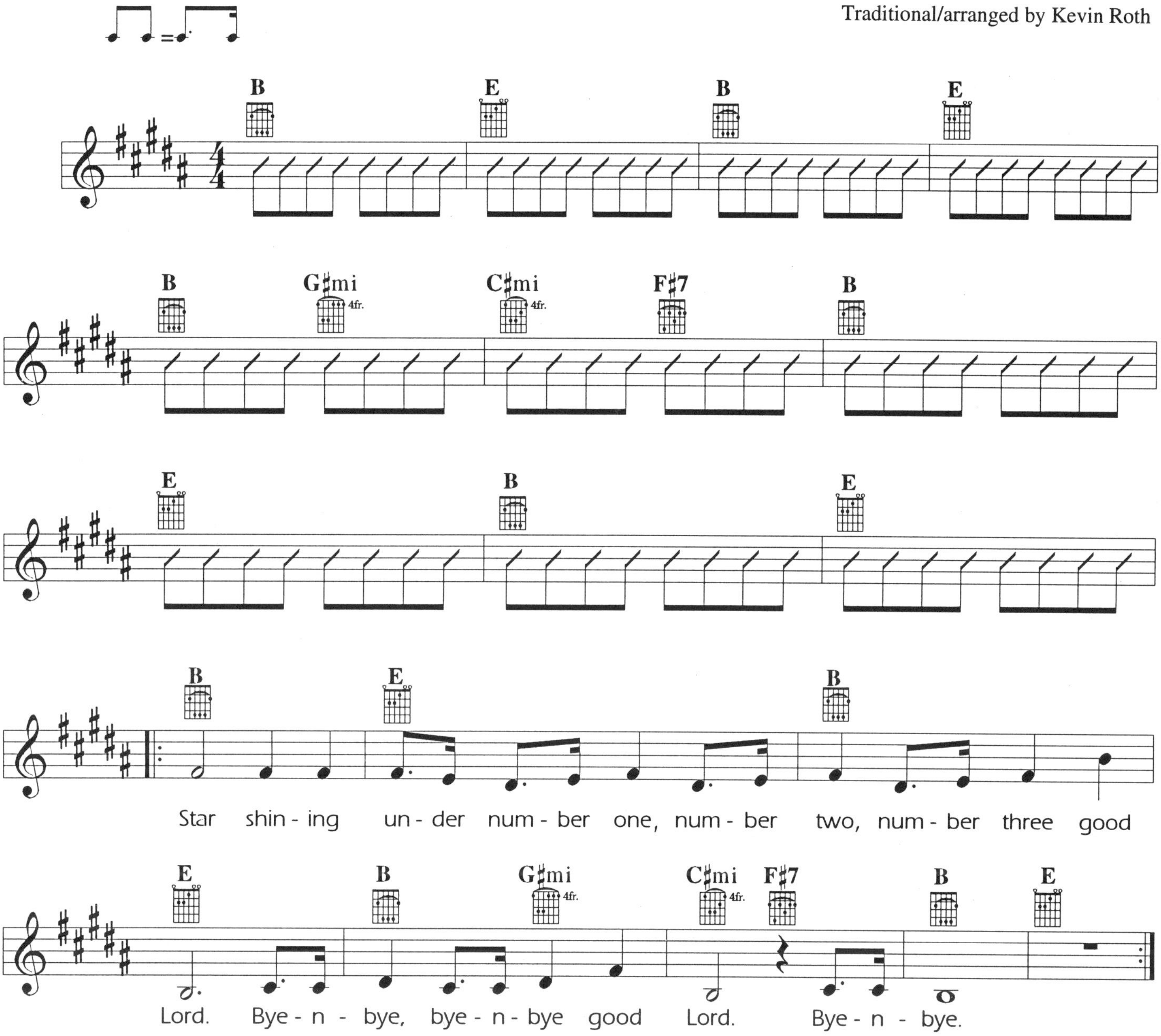

Star shining under number one, number two, number three good Lord
Bye 'n bye, bye 'n bye, good Lord, bye 'n bye.

Star shining under number four, number five, number six good Lord
Bye 'n bye, bye 'n bye, good Lord, bye 'n bye.

Star shining under number seven, number eight, number nine good Lord
Bye 'n bye, bye 'n bye, good Lord, bye 'n bye.

The Quiet Times

This song reminds us that there is a place we can go when our lives are out of balance, find our souls, (Our "higher self"), and find an inner peace.

by Kevin Roth

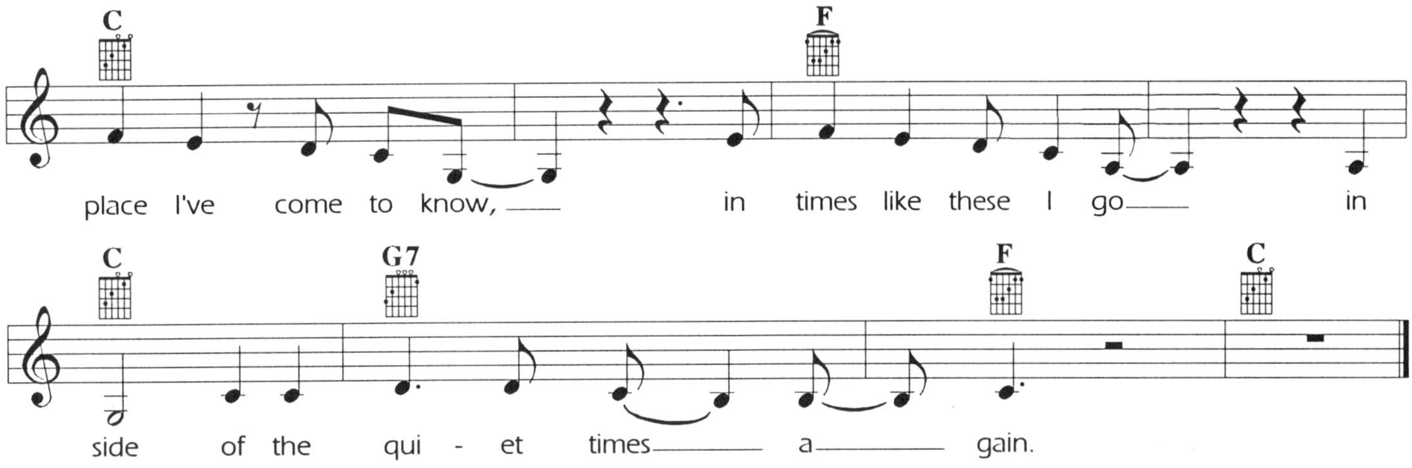

Chorus
Lullaby your cares away
Think good thoughts and good things will happen
Rest your mind and things will pass in time
I know they will, there's magic in the quiet times, they say

Take your troubles and your pain
All your worries and your blame
Take your life that's torn apart and come with me
To a place I've come to know
In times like these I go
Inside of the quiet times again

Chorus

The old folks from the hills
Lived a life of peace and fortune
Not for money or for riches did they care
But for love, good crops and a blue sky
With a prayer of thanks and blessing
Far richer for the quiet times they shared

Chorus

Take a lesson from this world
It's a world too fast for dreamers
Still there are some things that a man can never change
Like the blowing of the wind
Or the laughter of the children
And knowing there's a quiet time to find your soul again

Chorus

More *"Western Music"* books

from Centerstream Publications
P. O. Box 5450 - Fullerton, CA 92635

Songs Of The Trail
compiled by Ron Middlebrook
foreword by Rusty Richards
Centerstream Publications
Cowboys have always held a special place in the hearts and imaginations of Americans. Images of riding bravely and happily into the sunset, fending off dangerous enemies, and singing around the campfire evoke a sense of pride and respect for a lifestyle nearly forgotten in this age of progress. Relive the days of the cowboys bringing the herds home in this interesting compilation of facts and music. 53 songs celebrate the life and times on the range by such noted writers as Doc Denning, Chris LeDoux, Rusty Richards, Roy Rodgers Jr., and others. Their music is an actual view into their daily adventures, tribulations and entertainment. This unique publication also features articles on black cowboys, cowgirls, cowboys' Spanish ancestry, and more.
$14.95 • 9x12 • 112 pages • Softcover • • 0-9317-5967-6 • 00000152

SONGS 'ROUND THE CAMPFIRE

compiled by Ron Middlebrook
Centerstream Publications
96 of your favorite songs sung by "Hi" Busse, Tom Chambers, Robert Meyer, Dan Meyer, Tom Spaulding, Bob Wagoner, Buck Page, John Ryberg, John Lamount, Tex Ritter, and Carson Robinson. Also includes old cowboy photographs, a glossary of cowboy terms, bios of songwriters, Tumbleweed History, and more.
00000037..$24.95

Songs Of The Cowboy

Compiled by Ron Middlebrook
Centerstream Publications
This unique book celebrates the romance attached to the cowboy and his free roaming life style. By combining classic cowboy songs, trivia, photos, articles and diagrams with current cowboy songwriters' songs, this book pays special tribute to our Western musical heritage.
_______00000129...$12.95